Food Webs

by Grace Hansen

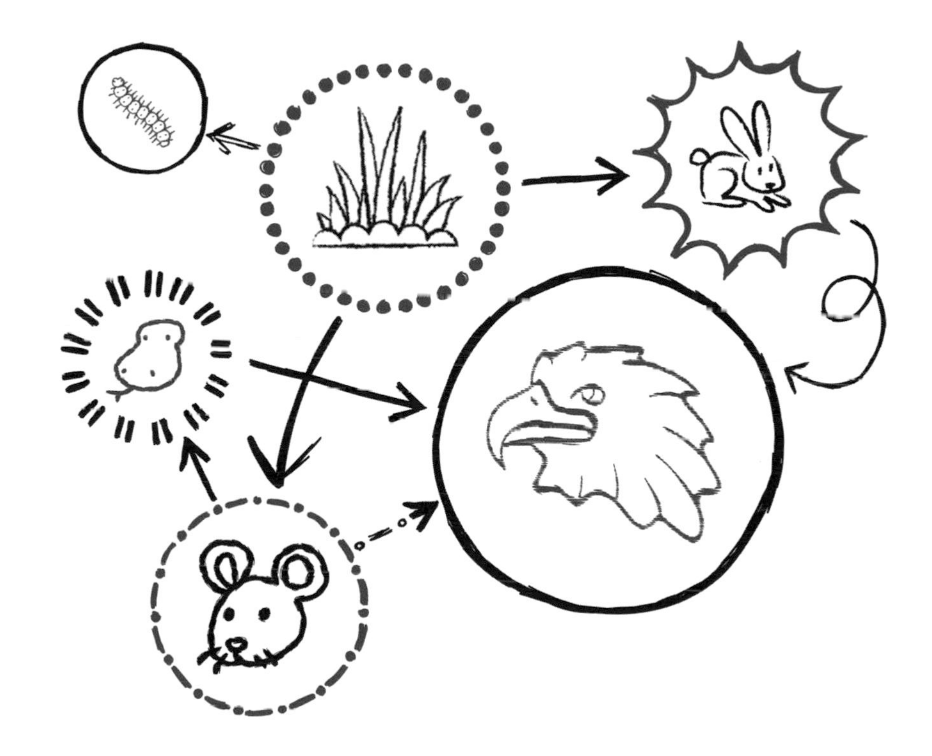

Abdo Kids
BEGINNING SCIENCE: ECOLOGY

Abdo Kids Jumbo is an Imprint of Abdo Kids
abdobooks.com

abdobooks.com

Published by Abdo Kids, a division of ABDO, P.O. Box 398166, Minneapolis, Minnesota 55439.

Printed in the United States of America, North Mankato, Minnesota.

102019

012020

Photo Credits: iStock, Science Source, Shutterstock

Production Contributors: Teddy Borth, Jennie Forsberg, Grace Hansen
Design Contributors: Dorothy Toth, Pakou Moua

Library of Congress Control Number: 2019941232

Publisher's Cataloging-in-Publication Data

Names: Hansen, Grace, author.

Title: Food webs / by Grace Hansen

Description: Minneapolis, Minnesota : Abdo Kids, 2020 | Series: Beginning science: ecology | Includes online resources and index.

Identifiers: ISBN 9781532188954 (lib. bdg.) | ISBN 9781644942680 (pbk.) | ISBN 9781532189449 (ebook) | ISBN 9781098200428 (Read-to-Me ebook)

Subjects: LCSH: Food webs (Ecology)--Juvenile literature. | Biomes--Juvenile literature. | Natural communities--Juvenile literature. | Ecology--Juvenile literature. | Food supply--Juvenile literature.

Classification: DDC 577.16--dc23

Table of Contents

What Is a Food Web?

To understand food webs, it is important to know about food chains. Food chains show how energy flows through an **ecosystem**.

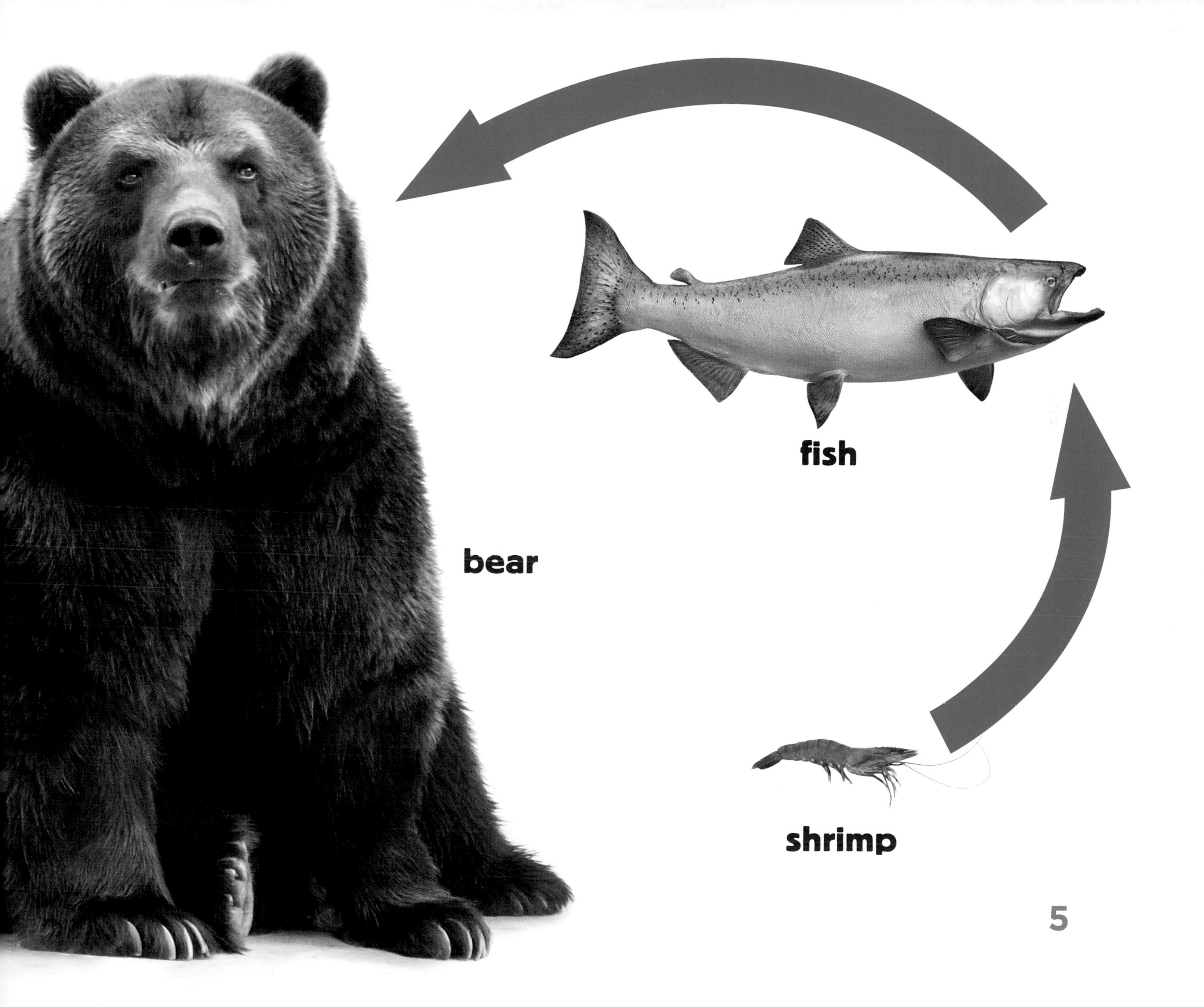
fish
bear
shrimp

Plants and animals are alive. Water and rocks are not alive. But they can all live and **interact** in the same place. They are part of an **ecosystem**.

No matter how big or how small, all living things need energy to survive. Living things get energy by eating.

Living things are grouped into three main categories in a food chain. Plants are producers. They make their own food to get energy.

Animals and humans are consumers. They must eat other living things for energy.

Decomposers are nature's recyclers. They clean up any leftover **waste**. They put nutrients back into the soil.

This flow of energy makes up a food chain. There are many different food chains in one **ecosystem**. These food chains can overlap. This makes a food web.

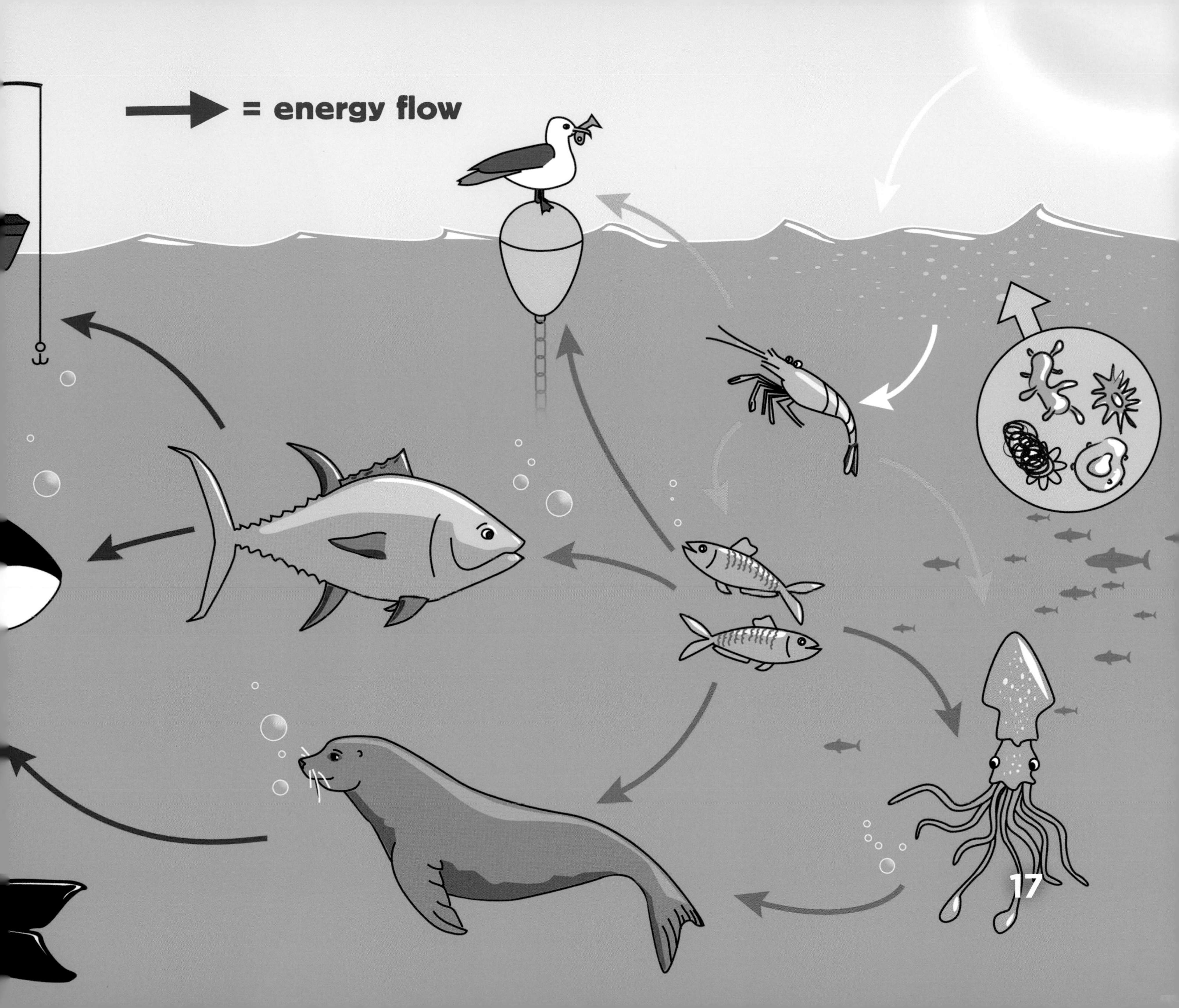
= energy flow

Rainforest Food Web

The Amazon Rainforest is filled with millions of plant, animal, and insect **species**. Each one of these things is a part of a food web.

Plants in the Amazon Rainforest are producers. Many animals and insects eat a plant's leaves, fruits, and seeds. Predators in the rainforest eat other animals. They all connect to form a food web.